A Fluttering of Wings

Graphics
by
Penny Havard

First Printing .... October, 1994
Second Printing ...... December, 1994
Third Printing .... October, 1995
Fourth Printing .... October, 1996
Fifth Printing .... March, 1998
Sixth Printing .... May, 2000

A Publication of
GRENFELL READING CENTER
Books in Print - Books on Tape
P.O. Box 98, 36 Narramissic Drive
Orland, Maine 04472-0098
Tel: 1-207-469-7102
Email: clarine@aol.com

Library of Congress Copyright © 1994
Hazel Andrews Morrison

ISBN 0-9612766-4-9

Printed in the United States of America by
Furbush-Roberts Printing Co., Inc.

A Fluttering of Wings

Hazel Andrews Morrison

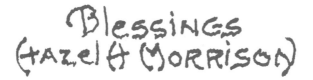

Blessings
(Hazel A Morrison)

Miss Hazel Grace Andrews, 1915

CONTENTS

MATURITY

OLD AGE

THE TIME

For Hazel
On publishing a book of verse at 104

She spins for us (knowing the time must come)
Entwining lines of verse, a chrysalis
Of captured memories —
                                        mud pies, sun-baked . . .
Sailboats on dancing seas . . . a walk along
A garden path . . . rainbows . . . candles puffed out
On flickering birthday cakes. . . .

                                Through all our years —
Childhood and youth, maturity, old age —
Slowly, laboriously, we creep about
Earthbound, longing for higher things.

                                        Time brings
A fluttering of wings — bright yellow? gold?
Deep purple? black? pale lavender? Who knows?

So patiently against the coming grief
She weaves page after page — enfolding strands
Of laughter and of tears, her loves, her life —
And leaves for us this shield of sheltering words.

Unfold it gently . . . hold it in your hands . . .
(Soon comes the time, the glorious time to fly!)
Hold it within your heart — and search the sky.

Autumn, 1994   Clarine Coffin Grenfell

FOREWORD

The encouragement, interest, and advice of my dear friend, Clarine Coffin Grenfell of Orland, Maine, have made *A Fluttering of Wings* possible. I am deeply indebted to her for her gifts of time and experience. Her introductory poem, "The Time," is a beautiful expression of the values I treasure.

How did our friendship begin? Shortly before leaving Bethel, Connecticut, in 1985. I was invited to a Book Club reading at the home of my friend, Louise Trimpert. Clarine was the guest of honor. We were entranced as she read from her delightful books of prose and poetry.

All of us could relate to stories of her life as a minister's wife in Bethel many years before. We laughed over the account of her own wedding, next door to an auction, as well as that of famous singer, Marian Anderson, from the book entitled *Women My Husband Married*.

In the decade since, I have ordered and re-ordered copies of this book for friends across the country. Sometimes with the orders I surprised Clarine by enclosing verses I had composed on sleepless nights. Imagine my amazement (and amusement) when she — at one time an editor at prestigious *Reader's Digest* — suggested I publish a book!

"Put your money," she wrote, "into something your grands and great-grands can hold in their hands and say, 'My Gram did this!' They can't do that with a tomb-stone!" Thank you, thank you, Clarine, for editorial guidance all along the way — from International Standard Book Numbers and Library of Congress copyright to eliminating dead words.

My heartfelt thanks, too, to Penny Havard of Rowayton, Connecticut, for her artistic graphite pencil drawing, the frontispiece in my book. Who would not want to be remembered this way — young, happy, idealistic, beginning a teaching career that was to last seven decades!

I first saw Penny Havard's work when her mother, Bertha Breidenbach, was a gifted student in my 'Kitchen Studio.' Penny's artistic ability was evident even then though she was

11

only a child. It has been my great pleasure to watch that talent develoip as she became a successful artist. Thank you, Penny, for your most generous gift.

Especially I want to thank my daughter Carol for her staunch support in this project. She answered my questions, helped me search for meaningful words, and encouraged me to 'stick with it.' Carol, through the years you have given me many gifts. This is one of your best — helping me make my dream a reality . . . seeing *A Fluttering of Wings* in print.

Finally to my readers — I hope you have as much pleasure reading this book of verse as I have had in writing it. Only 'verse,' I am well aware, not 'serious poetry,' but perhaps in the verses you will find my philosophy of life, expressed long ago in a poem by Henry Van Dyke. I give it to you on the following page in the calligraphy I so love to do.

San Jose, California
Autumn, 1994

*   *   *

A second printing within two months and now, nine months later, a third! The past year has truly been 'the year of the butterfly' — one of the happiest, most exciting years of my life. Thank you, readers in forty states and seven countries! I am grateful to you all and to the Good Lord who gives us this wonderful life.

September, 1995

*   *   *

A 4th printing for my 106th birthday! Twenty-seven more verses than in the first printing two years ago! All over Planet Earth — Maine to California, Florida to Alaska, New Zealand to Canada, Germany to Zimbabwe — some 2000 copies of my book being read!

The range of readership astonishes me — a pre-school class in Rhode Island sends illustrations of nature poems . . . a grieving son writes from Massachusetts: "Thank you for improving the quality of my mother's life in her last several months. *A Fluttering*

12

of Wings was on her table with her Bible when she died" . . . a gentleman in a nudist colony orders more copies for his friends . . . A Mormon clergyman entitles his Sunday sermon 'Live Like Hazel.'

At age 100, 101, 102, 103 I would not have dreamed such things possible. What marvelous surprises God has for us all along the way! With each new dawn I thank Him for the gift of this wonderful life and for family and loving friends with whom to share the swiftly passing days.

Autumn, 1996

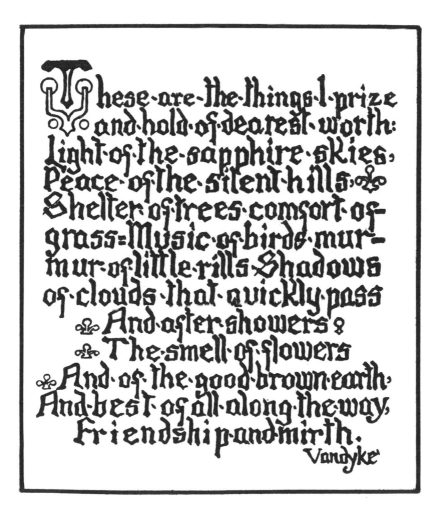

These are the things I prize and hold of dearest worth: Light of the sapphire skies, Peace of the silent hills, Shelter of trees, comfort of grass—Music of birds, murmur of little rills, Shadows of clouds that quickly pass, And after showers, The smell of flowers And of the good brown earth, And best of all along the way, Friendship and mirth.

Vandyke

Photo courtesty of Louise Trimpert

The First Congregational Church in Bethel, Connecticut, has long honored Hazel Andrews Morrison, confirmed in 1902, as its oldest member. The Reverend Mr. Marshall Linden was officiant and many lifelong friends were among the celebrants at a Service of Death and Resurrection in memory and celebration of her life held here March 17, 1998.

Family members coming from ten different states included son Samuel Morrison, Connecticut; daughter Caroline Morrison Garrett, California; grandchildren Martha Vermuth, Utah; Bill Morrison, Tennessee; Susan Rodis-Jones, Virginia; Beth Morrison, Kansas; Rob Garrett, Oregon; Bob Morrison, Texas; Betsy Morrison, Colorado; and Nancy Morrison, Florida.

The people of her home town and home church were always in Hazel's prayers, as reflected in one of her last poems:

INVITATION

Music of Sunday church bells sanctifies the air –
Divine invitation to join in praise and prayer
1997

14

Childhood

"Happiness is a butterfly,
which, if pursued,
is quite beyond your grasp,
but,
if you will sit down quietly,
may alight upon you."

Nathaniel Hawthorne

A JOYOUS CHILDHOOD

I remember as a child
       Wings upon my feet,
Breezes blowing through my hair
       While skipping down the street.

A song was vibrant in my heart!
       Music filled my ears!
"I hope, I hope, I hope," I sang,
       I live a thousand years!"

MY EARLIEST MEMORY

It was more than a hundred years ago,
       But I remember it still —
Watching, while sitting on Papa's knee,
The lamplighter's horse
       amble over the hill. . . .

WHY?

Why do cats have whiskers?
Why do dogs have tails?
What does an elephant hide in his trunk?
Why are snails named snail?

Why won't they answer my questions?
Why do they always say,
"You'll know when you grow older.
Now run along and play!"

                                        1996

16

LOW TIDE

Looking back on my childhood,
The days I truly prize
Are those I spent on sandbars
Left by outgoing tides.

Clam shells, moon shells, oyster shells,
Tumbled seaweed in wild disarray,
Hermit crabs, their homes on their backs –
All shared tidepools with minnows at play.

Excitement! I'd found a starfish,
A gift tossed up by the sea,
Resembling a star from the sky above
In a story once told to me –

A lonely star seeking adventure
Looked down on a sandbar one day,
Slid into the sea on a rainbow . . .
Once there, he decided to stay!

Perhaps I would see a mermaid –
I knew they must be nearby.
Sand dollars made me curious –
What were they planning to buy?

I wanted to linger there longer,
Searching for one treasure more,
But the incoming tide gave me warning –
Time to scurry ashore!

CONCERT

Peepers in the springtime!
Crickets in the fall!
Katydids and whippoorwills –
Nature's musicale!

17

THE LITTLE ANDREWS SISTERS

Sister Pauline was smaller than I.
We ran hand in hand down the street,
Dressed in playtime pinafores,
High-buttoned shoes on our feet.

She begged me to push her higher
On the swing Papa hung from a tree.
We made mud pies, baked them in the sun.
I was four . . . she was only three.

18

COCK-O-DOODLE-DO

One sound I miss in the morning
That thrilled me years ago
Is the rusty voice of the rooster
As he learned how to crow.

He'd strut around the barnyard,
His lordly comb held high,
Open his bill, flap his wings,
Then make another try.

The hen, demure and modest,
Put on much less of a show –
She'd lay her egg, jump from the nest,
Only cackle to let the world know.
1997

WHO DID IT?

I heard them in the evening,
Their voices clear and shrill,
Calling for a volunteer
To "Whip-poor-Will!"

The girl who chose to do it
Was a little prig,
And all her friends were tattle-tales,
Shouting, "Katy did! Katy did!"

CHOICE

Had I been born an insect
The one I'd like to be
Is the little, darting, lightning bug,
For it always seems to me
They have such fun with their tiny sparks,
Playing hide-and-go-seek in the evening dark!

19

A STORY
For Sarah, Eileen, and Emily

You want me to tell you a story?
    Well, once I was little like you.
I loved to visit my grandmother,
    The very same way you do.

She'd read me my favorite stories.
    After that, we'd go for a walk.
Sometimes we'd meet a friend of hers.
    I'd stand while they talked — and talked.

Then when the day was over,
    After all the 'good nights' had been said,
We'd play I was her bunny
    As we hippity-hopped to bed.

Oh, how I loved her pillows,
    Soft feathers, so snugly, so warm!
While rain made music on the roof —
    I knew I was safe from harm.

As Grandmother gave me a goodnight kiss,
    I'd hear her softly say,
"Sweet dreams, little darling! Tomorrow
    We'll have another nice day!"

TRADITION

Struggling bonsai trees
footbound like maidens of old
preserve tradition.

Youth

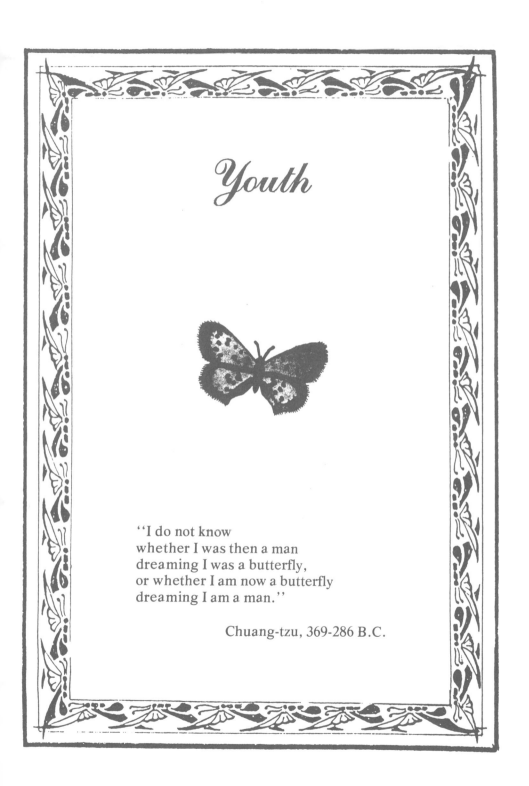

"I do not know
whether I was then a man
dreaming I was a butterfly,
or whether I am now a butterfly
dreaming I am a man."

Chuang-tzu, 369-286 B.C.

A happy day! Miss Hazel Andrews graduates from Bethel High School and is off to study art at famed Pratt Institute in Brooklyn, NY — known then as 'the City of Churches!'

CONFUSION

Emerging from confining cocoons,
*   Colorful butterflies*
Spread their wings in confusion —
*   So many ways to fly!*

MIRACLES

Everything in the world I see —
*   A breath-taking sunset,*
*   A small buzzing bee,*
*   Frost on a roof top,*
*   Snow on a pine —*
Each one a miracle,
*   Each one a sign*
That God's in His heaven.

*   Yet — He is so near . . .*
I have nothing to doubt.
*   I have nothing to fear.*

MORNING SONG

Walking early one morning
*   Along the village street,*
I hear a familiar serenade —
*   The song is 'tweet, tweet, tweet.'*

I think as the bird flies out of sight
*   What a happy world this would be*
If everyone sang in the morning
*   As this little bird sings to me.*
*   1995*

MISTY MORNING ON CAPE COD

Leaden the sea,
Leaden the sky,
Leaden the sailboats drifting by.
Fog this morning
Blew in to stay,
Draping the world in a shroud of gray.

Oh! How I wish
You were here with me
Wrapped in the gray of the misty sea,
Watching phantom gulls
Winging their way
High in the air above crashing spray!

TICK TOCK

What is time? Tick . . . tock . . .
Where does it go? Tick . . . tock . . .
Sometimes rushing past too fast —
Ticktockticktockticktock!
Sometimes creeping painfully slow —
Tick...tock...tick...tock...tick...tock....

Once yesterday was tomorrow!
Tomorrow will soon be today!
Today is NOW — a priceless gift!
Do not throw it away!
                                    1995

24

SEASCAPE

Lapping waves roll endlessly on
Caressing the sandy beach,
While a hungry gull patrols from above
For a clam within his reach.

MOTION

Trysting tide and moon
above a turbulent sea
happy in motion.

DANCE OF THE SURF

Each line of the surf is a ruffle
On the petticoat of the ocean,
While dancing steps of sea nymphs
Keep up the rhythmic motion.

I wonder who's giving the party
Causing all this commotion!

Pemaquid, Maine

25

Because of college and World War I, Hazel's engagement to high school sweetheart Garfield "Bob" Morrison lasted ten long years — "Ten years of romantic engagement," Hazel tells us, "followed by thirty-one years of romantic marriage!"

Here in 1918 a decorous Miss Andrews journeys from Connecticut to South Carolina to bolster the morale of her serviceman fiance, an instructor in the use of small arms at Camp Hancock.

GOD'S RAINBOW

Today God painted a rainbow,
Then hung it out to dry –
A spectrum of radiant color
On His clothesline in the sky.

SWEETHEARTS

Strolling the moonlit garden,
Fingers closely entwined,
We spun gossamer dreams of the future,
Dreams to come true with time.

The warp was the mist in the valley;
The woof, silver threads from a star –
With never a scissor to cut the thread,
Never a stain to mar.
1918

SIPPING

Butterflies circling the garden
Lit here and there as they flew,
Sipping from each tempting flower
Sweet nectar – a heady brew!

27

SUMMER AT KIMWOOD

There's a summer cottage anchored
On a ledge above the sea,
Welcoming each friend and neighbor
To its hospitality.

Every morning in the beauty
Of a new exciting dawn,
Waking birds in trees and thickets
Lift their hearts in grateful song.

Lapping tides along the coastline
Of the whitecapped summer sea
Joined by graceful, grey-winged seagulls
Swell the morning symphony.

Here the shoreline's fringed with pine trees
High above the rocky beach
Where low blueberry bushes
And sweet wild roses meet.

Nature's paint brush, always busy,
Mixes colors, clear or gray,
Holding daily exhibitions
On the land and o'er the bay.

Maturity

"The leaves fall early this autumn. . . .
The paired butterflies are already
            yellow with August
Over the grass in the West garden;
They hurt me. I grow older."

Ezra Pound

Mr. and Mrs. Garfield Morrison

UNION

Slanting lines of rain,
pines glimpsed through mist — dream etchings,
unite earth, sea, sky.

APRIL CHALLENGE

Come watch with me at the window
    The artistry of rain,
Singing a song of water
    Running down the window pane.

The misty grayness of the day
    Adds beauty to the scene,
Challenging the raindrops
    To clothe the world in green.

Melting snows of winter
    Answer April's call,
Cascading down the mountain
    In musical waterfall.

Beauty awakens in April,
    Kissed by sun and shower,
Challenging the landscape
    To burst from bud to flower.

SUMMER SHOWER

Beneath the arch of a rainbow,
    Splashed by cooling rain,
From mountain top to placid sea
    Colors grow vibrant again.

HAPPINESS

Happiness is Homewood!
    Come sit awhile with me
Where the summer breezes play
    Castanets in the tall oak tree.

There's a farflung view across the bay —
    Each island etched in green,
Lazily drifting pleasure craft
    Beckoning in between.

As long as memory lingers,
    I shall treasure every day
You and I spent together
    At Homewood on the bay.

ANOTHER WORLD

Homewood on Drinkwater Point
    Is a happy place to be
Where cottages sit sunning
    On the bluff above the sea.

Across diamond-dusted waters
    Sparkling paths lead straight to Spain,
Except for friendly islands
    To remind us we're in Maine.

We awaken in the morning
    To the music of the tide,
Circling gulls above the shoreline
    Where little chipmunks hide.

It's another world we live in,
    And we're very sure to find,
When vacation days are ended,
    We've left our hearts behind.

                              Yarmouth, Maine

32

THE BUTTERFLY BALLET

A sun-drenched day to remember!
The ballet a dazzling surprise!
Dancing airily into my garden
A host of butterflies!
Monarchs black and orange
Lead the troupe of delicate hue,
A rainbow of living color —
Pink, yellow, green, violet, blue!

Flower beds bright with blossoms
Set the stage where they dip and soar,
Awaiting melodious songbirds
To orchestrate their score.
Awestruck with admiration,
Mute audience of one,
I watch as they take their positions —
The ballet has begun!

Ballerinas, quivering, darting,
Poise gracefully in air,
Hover over the swaying flowers
With choreographic flair.
Now the glorious Grand Finale!
Beneath a sapphire sky,
Gauzy wings spread wide in the sunlight,
They ascend as one buterfly!

Afternoon shadows lengthen. . . .
The fluttering corps take flight,
Bending low, they blend with the blossoms,
Then disappear from sight!
I clap my hands as they exit
This breezy summer day,
Applauding the wondrous performance
Of the Butterfly Ballet!
105th Birthday Poem
Autumn, 1995

MATHEMATICS
For Sherman, age ten

I had reasoned with Sherman, age ten,
Why he should be at his best
When we were having dinner that night
With the minister as our guest.

No rushing to the table
Before all of us were there!
No interrupting conversation!
No tilting back the chair!

For once he had remembered
To do as he'd been told
Till he and the Reverend Dunham
Each reached for the last raised roll.

"How many rolls have you had, sir?"
The minister answered, "Three."
"Well, I have eaten only two,
So this last one belongs to me."

When I returned from the kitchen
Where I had gone for more,
I saw our little gentleman
Disappearing through the door.

I thought with some amusement
As our son ran down the path,
"If he ever becomes a professor,
I'm sure that he'll teach math!"

THE HOOK
For Sam

There's something I have always wished
But never told a soul —
That you would be a blacksmith, Sam,
Before you grew too old.

The postman brought a box today
With a message in your hand:
"The first thing I have ever made!
For Ma, from Blacksmith Sam!"

"Ye gods!" I said to Carol.
"Come and take a look!
Your brother Sam, the Blacksmith,
Has sent a great big hook!

"We'll place it in the living room!"
"Oh, no, we won't!" said she.
"We'll put it in the kitchen.
That's where it ought to be!"

She found a nail to hang it,
And there upon the hook
Resides my favorite coffee mug —
You'll see it if you look.

It's not hard to understand
How filled with joy I am!
At last I have a Blacksmith Son —
And his name is Sam!

Hazel and Garfield enjoyed travel to many parts of the world. Here in 1935 they set out on a cruise to South America.

CYPRESS

Twisted and gnarled and rugged they stand —
*   The cypress of Monterey,*
Buffeted by ocean winds,
*   Refreshed by fog and spray.*

Undaunted through centuries of time,
*   Guarding the bluffs and the bay,*
A marvel of nature's handiwork —
*   The cypress of Monterey.*

REDWOODS

Today I walked in the redwoods
*   Where trees of gigantic size*
Have weathered a thousand years,
*   Towering to meet the skies.*

I felt so inconsequential,
*   Wandering on my way,*
'Til I saw a tiny white blossom,
*   Proud to be on display.*

I stood in the presence of beauty —
*   Ancient trees and new-blown flower —*
Thanking my God for the gift of sight
*   And an unforgettable hour.*

SAN FRANCISCO

Glistening roof tops,
a mosaic of beauty,
hide life's tragedies.

GOLDEN GATE BRIDGE

Like a spider web
the bridge above the blue bay
connects land with land.

CAPTAIN

The bell buoy sounds its warning dirge,
The Captain masters the spray,
Charting his ship forthrightly
Into welcoming arms of the bay.

OCTOBER GLORY

I've been to an exhibition today —
One a critic could never defy.
The canvas stretched from east to west,
Bounded by earth and sky.

The palette, brilliant with colors,
Thrilled me beyond belief,
Turning the landscape from green to gold,
Not skipping a single leaf.

I wondered, awestruck by such beauty,
How artists dare even try
To duplicate in their limited way
This glory of earth and sky.

The Master whose hand has wrought it
And given us eyes to see
Looks down from above and with brushes of love
Fills our hearts with ecstasy.

APPRECIATION

How can I thank you, dear old World,
For pleasures you share with me—
Majesty of mountains,
Song of surging sea,
Seasons rich in color —
Springtime, summer, fall,
Cold blue shadows of winter —
I am grateful for them all.

1995

Hazel's Victorian home at 220 Greenwood Avenue, Bethel, not far from her birthplace. Here in 1950 she established her celebrated 'Kitchen Studio,' running it with great success until 1985, her 95th year.

A TEACHER'S HEART

The toleware class is meeting!
Eager students rush through my door!
Arms overflowing with flowers and lunch,
They bring projects unfinished before.

Gladys Shepard, first to join the class,
Will paint only one piece, she makes clear,
But when Aunt Mary's tray is such a success,
She continues — for thirty more years!

Word spreads to Brookfield and Newtown,
Bridgeport, New Haven, too.
They arrive from Wilton and Redding
With treasures their grandmothers knew —

Mirrors, boxes, one rocking chair,
Battered trays, a quaint antique clock.
In no time at all my orderly house
Resembles a second-hand shop.

We paint, laugh, and chat together.
Friendships grow deep from the start.
I marvel to think of the talents unleashed —
Rewards for a teacher's heart.

RICHES

I do not have banknotes in thousands
Nor treasures appraisers rank high.
Yet my 'assets' run in the millions
That never a dollar could buy.

I'm grateful for birdsong in treetops,
For the cooling splash of rain,
For the sun that shines in my window,
For flowers that bloom in the lane . . .

For forest-clad valleys and mountains,
Home of the fleet-footed deer,
For the beauty of each new season
That adds to my pleasure each year . . .

For gulls gliding over the beaches
Where waves caress the shore,
And sandpipers dart as if running a race
With the surf they seem to ignore . . .

For neighbors I chat with while walking,
For children whose laughter I share,
For artistic friends who inspire me,
Make me rich as a millionaire . . .

For the charm of the evening sunset,
For the stars that shine in the sky —
I'm thankful for all of these 'assets'
That money could never buy.

My cup runneth over with blessings.
I count them again and again —
The love and devotion of family,
The love and devotion of friends.

Old Age

"When thou dost ask me blessing,
                    I'll kneel down,
And ask of thee forgiveness.
                    So we'll live,
And pray, and sing, and tell old tales,
                    and laugh
At gilded butterflies . . .
And take upon's the mystery of things
As if we were God's spies,
                    and we'll wear out
Packs and sets of great ones."

Shakespeare, *King Lear*

MY SECRET

Folks are always asking me
The cause of my longevity.
There is just one — I know 'tis true —
I'll pass the secret on to you:

The year was eighteen-ninety,
A cold November day.
The stork stopped by and left me,
Then quickly flew away.

ADVICE AT EIGHTY-NINE

Never go to dances!
Never hurry, jog, or climb!
Advice comes to me daily
Now that I'm eighty-nine!

I know I could twirl in a waltz again,
Run to catch a bus on time!
No need to sit upon the shelf —
I'm only eighty-nine!

If you think that I am fooling,
Try to follow me sometime.
You'll find you're the one that's winded,
Even though I'm eighty-nine!

When I get to be a hundred,
Such advice will be just fine.
I may be ready then for a rocking chair,
But not at eighty-nine!

LISTEN TO THE MOCKING BIRD

A young and talented mocking bird
    Hides in our orange tree,
Regaling me every morning
    With his musical harmony.

He practices over and over
    The songs he loves to sing,
Mimicking all the other birds
    With their overtures to spring.

I listen with rapt attention
    To his lovely roundelay
Before he glides to another tree
    For his afternoon matinee.

GIFTS

Among rare gifts from nature
    One that I dearly prize
Is the dancing, fleeting movement
    Of exquisite butterflies.

IN STYLE AT NINETY

They tell me I am ninety years old.
Well, I know it's a fact,
But I always thought at this ripe old age
That I'd be dressed in black —

A black silk dress with a fichu of lace,
A cameo at my throat,
With a little lace doily atop my head
Like the pictures in Godey's Book.

I thought I'd sit in a rocking chair
With a foot stool under my feet,
Sipping cambric tea to comfort me
And make the picture complete.

But now that I've reached ninety,
There's no black dress in my dreams.
In fact, I am longing to model
A pair of those tight-fitting jeans!

CARROUSEL

Many looked on with envy
When alluring Ruth with her charm
Announced on her ninetieth birthday
A protector to keep her from harm.

Her friends were filled with excitement!
She'd be spending the rest of her life
With a gentleman who'd told her
He longed to make her his wife!

Each picked a brass-ring winner
In the carrousel of life.
Now Howard's her happy husband,
And Ruth, his dutiful wife.

HONESTY

There's a story I like to tell
*   About my sister and me*
Of a photo taken long ago
*   When we were two and three.*

The postman left some reprints,
*   Then hurried on his way*
As Mrs. Ludlow, the laundress,
*   Was finishing for the day.*

"Mrs. Ludlow, let me show you
*   My sister Pauline and me*
In a picture taken years ago
*   When we were two and three."*

"What pretty little girls!" she sighed,
*   Then turned her attention to me —*
The remark she made in doleful tones
*   A triumph of honesty:*

"Now ain't it true, Miz Morrison,
*   What so often people say?*
If you're pretty when you're little
*   You never grow up that way."*
*   1995*

TODAY'S THE DAY

Long ago I thought no age
    Could rival sweet sixteen,
And then, when I turned twenty-one,
    I thought that was the cream.

But now I know beyond a doubt
    Today's the day to shout about,
For I'm as thrilled as I can be
    To tell the world I'm ninety-three!

A CHRISTMAS RAINBOW

Two little girls leave a gift for me,
    A really beautiful sight to see —
A rainbow painted with colored chalk
    Twenty feet long on my wide front walk!

Some people might have been annoyed,
    But to me it is choicest art —
A present money could never buy,
    A Christmas gift from the heart.

Though rains will come, as they always do,
    And wash all the beauty away,
I will never forget the happiness
    Given me this Christmas Day.

DAFFODIL WAY

Looking out of my window,
  What do I see?
A turquoise blue sky
  Smiling at me.

A bird flying past
  Darts low, flies high
Viewing each tree
  With an architect's eye.

Red pyracantha,
  Cascading the fence,
Vie with the fuchsias,
  Both colors intense.

Blossoms, exquisite
  As carved ivory,
Fall in profusion
  From the white plum tree.

So thick are they clustered,
  Above and below,
They give the effect
  Of a new-fallen snow.

Tulip and hyacinth,
  Fragrant and gay,
Enhance springtime's pageant
  On Daffodil Way.

TRAVELER

I am a rocking-chair traveler,
My trusty walker near —
No thought of heavy luggage,
No rainy-weather gear.

I need no map for a travel guide.
I'll always be on time—
No rush to get to the starting gate,
No back-breaking stairs to climb.

What did I hear the announcer say —
We'll be in Rome tonight?
That will be fun to think about
When I put out the light.

Rome with all its glory,
Paintings beyond compare,
Will set the pace for my journey
As I rock back and forth in my chair.

Next I'll think of Florence,
A wonderful city to see,
Steeped in unrivaled beauty,
Deep in antiquity.

From Florence I'll travel to Venice
To see where the glass is made,
Glide over streets of water
In gondolas, unafraid.

Then north to the Alps I'll travel —
What breathtaking views arise,
As lofty peaks with earthbound feet
Reach upward to the sky!

Now it's goodbye to Europe
    For the loveliest night of all —
I'll stand in the moonlight of summer
    Viewing the Taj Mahal.

With each of you 'dear travelers'
    My trip I'll gladly share.
Surprise and adventure await us
    From the depths of an old rocking chair.

EVENING IN PARIS

A festive night in Paris
    Under the moon and stars.
We sit at a cafe table,
    Nibbling crackers with caviar.

Dubonnet sparkles in glasses,
    A most refreshing treat.
As we sip, we are serenaded
    By musicians, strolling the street.

Patrons of art in passing
    Enjoy paintings on display —
The work of hungry artists,
    Hoping for sales each day.

What pleasure day dreams offer
    As we travel near and far
To cities of distinction —
    Artistic, romantic, bizarre!

1996

51

ESKIMO'S DARLING

I'm on my way to Alaska,
A new career to pursue —
To be an Eskimo's darling
And live as Eskimos do.

If this life is not to my liking,
I'll board the next ship for the States —
Leave him alone in his igloo
To find a more suitable mate.

Princess Cruise, 1987

During her many years, Hazel has been much more than a 'rocking chair traveler.' Here in 1987 at age 97 she sets out with Caroline on a Princess Cruise to Alaska.

LITTLE STAR

Little star shining in the sky,
When you look down on me,
Do I twinkle and sparkle as brightly for you
As you sparkle and twinkle for me?

HOSPITAL BIRTHDAY
For Caroline

A special day is a birthday
Because it is yours alone.
No one can take it from you,
No matter how old you've grown.

They whiz around much faster
When you're no longer a child –
Just think of your aged mother!
Her years have gone hogwild!

Once you get out of that tiresome bed,
You can shake your doctor's hand
And give him a thousand reasons
You think he's an awesome man.

You would not forget the nurses
Who have been so good to you.
May blessings follow them everywhere
In the wonderful work they do.

This greeting straight from a mother's heart
Comes with nothing but love and praise
For the daughter who from the day she was born
Has brightened each one of my days.
September 14, 1994

53

EXCITEMENT

Each year brings new excitement.
  This year it was a quake —
First a jolt, the floor rose up,
  The chairs began to shake.

A Chinese plate flew off the wall
  And shattered on the floor.
We were not hurt. Our loss was light.
  We thought it would be more.

After the earthquake, my birthday!
  Oh, what a wonderful time!
Bidding farewell to ninety-eight,
  Welcoming ninety-nine!

COBWEB

I watch a spider building her web,
  A gifted architect she,
Needing no blueprint to guide her,
  No apprentice for company.

She begins her web at the center —
  A classical design
Used through countless generations
  Since the beginning of time.

Now her artistry is finished,
  Every knot secure.
Patient, she waits for a victim
  To enter her cobweb lure.

  1995

MAKE BELIEVE
For Carol and Bob

Relaxing in a deck chair
On shipboard out at sea —
Is this a dream? or just a joke
Being played on you and me?

No alarm clock in the morning!
No traffic jams! No phones!
No bills to pay! No meals to get!
So far away from home!

We think we're going to stay here —
We've paid our costly fares —
And make believe for five more days
We're really millionaires!

SUMMER SUNSET

Clouds float high in the western sky,
At the close of a summer day,
Enriched by a glorious sunset,
A crimson and gold display.

Misty vapors arising
Reflect each muted hue,
Brilliant colors fading —
Shell pink, pearl grey, azure blue.

1995

55

November 22, 1990. The much-loved 'Celebrated Matriarch' — artist, teacher, poet, friend, mother of three, grandmother of nine, great-grandmother of seven — celebrates a hundred years of vigorous, joyous living!

"Happy Birthday, dear Hazel!" friends and family sing lustily, "Happy Birthday to you!"

LIFE EXPECTANCY

When I was ninety-six years old,
My doctor said to me,
"Now that you are ninety-six,
Your life expectancy
IS TWENTY MINUTES!"

I laughed and laughed until I ached —
No more time to celebrate?
I vowed that I would fool her,
AND TODAY I'M NINETY-EIGHT!

ONE HUNDRED YEARS OLD TODAY

This is the glorious morning
To celebrate as we may
The wonderful gift of living —
One hundred years old today!

Now as I stand on the summit
Where a hundred years have led,
I pay tribute to the 'good ole days,'
As I toast — the days ahead!

God, who holds the shuttle,
Weaving warp and woof of time,
Fashions the tapestry of each life
According to His design.

I hope when my pattern is finished,
When the last firm knot is tied,
He will welcome me into His Kingdom
And look on His work with pride.

STYLE SETTER

A sparkling morning in autumn!
  We decide to go for a ride.
Carol is waiting in the car,
  I walk down the path with pride.

"Why are you walking so funny?" she asks.
  "What do you mean, my dear?
I've walked the same way for a hundred years.
  Are you calling my footsteps queer?"

"Look down at your feet!" she says, smiling.
  I look. Can it really be true —
Two shoes made for the same foot,
  One brown, the other blue?

We burst into gales of laughter,
  Amused as we can be.
'It isn't often,' I think to myself,
  'Such a good joke is played on me.'

I hadn't noticed the difference,
  But no need to change shoes today,
This may be a style in the making!
  We go merrily on our way.

1996

58

CONVERSATION

I had the strangest dream last night —
    I hope, dear friend, it comes true!
A cigarette came to talk with me
    About his strong grip on you.

He said, "I knew I could get her
    After that very first puff.
If ever she tried to shake me,
    I'd certainly make it tough."

"You are very wrong," I said,
    Looking him straight in the eye.
"My friend comes from Yankee stock.
    She accomplishes what she tries."

Then I called him a robber.
    This made him mad as could be.
He said, "It's none of your business
    How much she spends on me!"

I told him, "Your smell is obnoxious —
    In the house, in her clothes, in her hair!
You fill the air with deadly fumes!"
    This made his temper flare.

He then made this assertion —
    "For years we've been best friends.
There is no doubt about it.
    I'll get her in the end!"

Then I dreamed I saw you, dear one,
    Triumphant, happy each day,
Enjoying the many years of life
    You almost threw away!

FIFTIETH ANNIVERSARY
For Sam and his beloved Betty

The very first time he met her
  His heart began to spin!
After a single game of chess,
  She was the girl for him!
Fifty years ago today
  She became his blushing bride —
He, in white dress uniform,
  Held her moist hand with pride.

The guests were all elated
  When the parson tied the knot —
Except for those who fainted!
  The day was hot hot hot!
In the Urbans' colorful garden
  They stood in line to greet
Perspiring friends who waited
  Despite the sultry heat.

Ducking into the basement,
  The men found a perfect spot
To down a drink with coolness
  And forget they were so hot.
Tables laden with pastries
  Caused wilting ladies to say,
"My, what a lovely reception —
  But, oh, what a fiendish day!"

They tarried too long at their party,
　　Then happily drove away
To the Roger Smith in Stamford
　　Where their room had been given away!
"You are late," the desk clerk thundered,
　　"But there's no need to panic.
There's one more room — 'neath a hot tin roof —
　　You can spend the night in the attic."

Now after fifty happy years
　　The story we gather to tell
Is of a marriage truly made in heaven
　　Despite the first night spent in —

Well, it certainly was hot!

ASSURANCE

From mountain peaks of gladness
Through valleys dark with sudness,
He holds my hand and leads me
Where faith's flowers grow.

Uplifting each day's living,
My straying thoughts forgiving,
Assuring me repeatedly
Of love's eternal flow.

1996

FRIENDSHIP

I walk with Sue in her garden
Down paths of exquisite color,
Each flower crowned to perfection,
Each adding joy to the hour —

Roses of breath-taking colors,
Lilies and snapdragons tall,
Johnny-jump-ups and pansies,
Sweet jasmine perfuming all.

A rug of brilliant impatience
At the foot of the white plum tree
Sparkles in dancing sunshine —
A delightful picture to see.

Daisies lining the pathway
Bow as we stroll by.
Stately blue delphinium
Reflect the summer sky.

As we sit in the cool gazebo,
Enjoying the summer air,
I think each fragrant blossom
Thanks Sue for her loving care.

Whatever happens tomorrow,
I will always remember the way
I walked with Sue in her garden
One wonderful day in May.

ROMANCE AT 102

I can't believe what I saw last night
*   When the moon went sailing by!*
I looked at him, he looked at me —
*   And winked at me with one eye!*

He saw that I was embarrassed,
*   Embarrassed as I could be,*
So then he winked his other eye —
*   Was he playing a joke on me?*

I guess he wants to date me,
*   But I find it strange as can be*
That the man in the moon in his travels
*   Would pick an old gal like me!*

COLORING BOOK

Green is the marshland
*   Where brown cattails grow*
And red-wing blackbirds
*   Fly to and fro.*

A crystal clear stream
*   Meandering by*
Mirrors the blue
*   Of the morning sky.*

Brilliant yellow cowslips
*   Highlight the show,*
Over the marshland
*   Where cattails grow.*

DIAGNOSIS

"Insomnia" — a problem for doctors!
To this I can never agree,
For wakeful nights
In God's beautiful dark
Are often a blessing to me!

Thoughts crowded out in daytime
Return with the stillness of night,
Bringing the inspiration
For verses I love to write.

A CELEBRATED MATRIARCH

It is with great humility
I admit to being one-hundred-and-three.
I do not dance,
I cannot sing,
Or cook or scrub a single thing.

In other ways I do relate —
At every meal I clean my plate.
Three naps a day
Keep me most fit,
And after them I read and sit . . . and sit. . . .

I am as proud as I can be
That I have reached one-hundred-and-three.
When all is said,
I do my part —
A celebrated matriarch!

ENCORE AT 104

Eva and Sandy and Lou today
Gave a 'Village House' luncheon for me
To celebrate my birthday —
A remarkable hundred-and-three!

A balloon attached to the back of my chair
Floated high above my head.
Everyone in the room could see,
"Happy Birthday" it proudly read.

I sat between Lou and Eva,
Two of my loving friends.
A guest at a table near us
Thought Eva and I were twins!

She turned toward her smiling friend,
Looked at Eva and then at me,
Then asked so very politely,
"Which one is one-hundred-and-three?"

Every crumb of the lunch was delicious,
Seasoned with laughter and glee.
I blew out the birthday candle
With a puff that surprised even me!

The gifts of love you brought me
Will add joy to many days more.
May I share with you my secret wish?
ENCORE at one-hundred-and-four!

MAY DAY

A bull frog sits on a lily pad
*   One breezy day in May,*
Winks at a passing dragon fly,
*   Who thinks he wants to play.*

The bull frog opens wide his mouth.
*   The dragon fly fears no hurt.*
But now her name's on the menu —
*   Favorite Frog Dessert.*

ADVICE FOR JOHN
On his buying a new Buick and a Persian rug

I have a friend who was told by a friend —
*   The same as I'm now telling you —*
"Go out and spend it! Have a good time!
*   You can't take your checkbook with you!"*

My friend sat down and pondered,
*   Puzzled early and late . . .*
How keep all the things she valued
*   And still reach Heaven's Gate?*

She itemized her treasures —
*   They numbered a thousand and two —*
Then went out and bought a U-HAUL-IT!
*   Will St. Peter let her through?*

1996

THIS GIFT OF LIVING

My one-hundred-and-fourth birthday —
A day of special thanksgiving,
For God in His infinite love
Gave me this gift of living.

From the peak of the years I have traveled,
Looking back from where I now stand,
Bright days, dark days, in-between days
Fit together with blessings He planned.

Joys have outnumbered sorrows,
Smiles have outnumbered tears
As truth will outdistance falsehood
And faith outdistance fears.

GRATITUDE

Sumac, red on the hillside,
Whitecaps, sparkling at sea —
All nature is vibrant with color,
Foretelling the winter to be.

Wild geese migrating southward
In a long graceful curve overhead,
Blue smoke curling from chimneys —
Reminders that summer has fled.

Had I only one day to ponder
The beauties and joy of the fall,
I would spend it praising my Master
For making me part of it all.

NATIONAL LEAGUE OF AMERICAN PEN WOMEN, INC.
Santa Clara County Branch

Upon the recommendation of the members
this Certificate of Appreciation is presented to

Hazel Andrews Morrison

in recognition for achievement in

Letters

Presented this day: October 7, 1995

President

Achievers Chairman

"One for all and all for one"

AN EXCITING MOMENT for Hazel Andrews Morrison occurred October 7, 1995, when she was presented with the Certificate of Appreciation Award from the Santa Clara County Branch of the *National League of American Pen Women, Inc.*

SPRING

Spring breezes in on tiptoe,
*   Fragrant flowers in her hair.*
Resplendent in rainbow colors,
*   Her beauty reigns every where.*

SUMMER

When temperatures soar in summer,
*   We long for a cooling breeze,*
Relax with a book for amusement
*   In the welcoming shade of a tree.*

FALL

In fall the leaves change color
*   From summer's dusty green.*
Flaming red, yellow, orange
*   Create autumn's perennial theme.*

WINTER

Through freezing nights of winter
*   Earth sleeps, snugly warm –*
Her eiderdown blanket of snowflakes,
*   A gift from the winter storm.*
*   1997*

YELLOW BIRD

The little bird was yellow.
    His tiny beak was black.
He lit upon my window sill,
    Looking for a snack.

Loitering but a moment,
    Suddenly he flew
To the topmost branch in the redwood
    Beneath skies of cobalt blue.

1996

HUMMING BIRD

What adulation the humming bird brings,
    Darting in flight on whirring wings —
Swift as an arrow released in air,
    Sampling the feeder's tempting fare!

1996

BLACKBIRD

Blackbirds are entertaining
    In my favorite mulberry tree,
Here at the end of the garden path
    Connecting my neighbor with me.

They arrived in flocks this morning,
    Each bringing a feathered friend.
Now the air is filled with chatter
    As their banquet draws to an end.

1996

JACK FROST

While I was snug asleep last night,
Jack Frost came with a pencil of white,
Drew pictures on the window pane —
Tall jagged mountains on icy terrain.

A rising sun made him hurry away —
No time to sign his picture today.
In biting cold as the moon shines bright,
He'll add his signature tonight.

1996

OUTSIDE AND IN

OUTSIDE, a nor'easter is howling —
Biting winds, blowing all night,
Drifting snow covers the landscape,
A world of ice frozen in white.

INSIDE, the cottage is cozy.
Contentment fills the air,
Blazing logs in the fireplace
Warm the cat curled asleep on the chair.

1996

71

SUMMER STORM

Dark clouds pile high in the western sky
This torrid afternoon.
The distant rumble of thunder
Promises showers soon.

Flashes of zigzag lightning
Play hide-and-seek in the rain.
Parched fields, scorched and thirsty,
Change from ochre to green again.

1996

MOMENTS OF GLORY

Leaves are changing color —
From green to crimson, gold,
Orange, brilliant yellow —
As the pageant of autumn unfolds.

Dancing leaves twirl in the sunshine,
Float from branches on high,
Perform to echoing music
From migrating birds flying by.

Brief fleeting moments of glory!
Beauty for all to share!
The gift of October dazzles —
Most memorable month of the year!

1996

TIME MARCHES ON

The question I'm most often asked,
Since I'm now one-hundred-and-five,
Is "To what do you attribute your age?"
I guess it's because I'm alive!
Yes, I was born in 1890 —
A long, long time to survive!

1996

GIFT

Come see my birthday coverlet,
A gift I highly prize,
A loving present from Clarine —
Woven butterflies!

Against a pearly white background —
The other side cherry red —
Butterflies hover profusely,
Lifelike in colored thread.

Under my butterfly coverlet
I like to nap each day,
Dreaming I fly on fluttering wings
In gardens where butterflies play!

MEMORIES

On golden wings of memory
*   I enjoy the years gone by,*
Grateful for every bonus day –
*   A gift at one-hundred-and-five!*

No need to sit and wonder
*   What each tomorrow brings.*
I live with friends of long ago
*   On memory's golden wings.*
*   1995*

ONE HUNDRED AND SIX

I'm a collector of birthdays,
*   A hobby many despise!*
For each year is invariably different,
*   With many a joyous surprise.*

Beginning in eighteen-ninety,
*   A century ago,*
I have not missed a single one.
*   How exciting to watch them grow!*

First there was only one digit.
*   Now a venerable three –*
One hundred and six, to be exact,
*   Astonishing even me!*
*   1996*

July 2, 1997

Mrs. Hazel Andrews Morrison
% Butterfly Books
811 Daffodil Way
San Jose, California 95117

Dear Mrs. Morrison:

　　Clarine Coffin Grenfell recently sent me a copy of your book, "A Fluttering of Wings". I am delighted to have this beautifully written collection of poems!

　　You are indeed an inspiration to those of us who are attempting to make the world a better place in which to live. In the cynical world of politics, it is refreshing to read the uplifting words of a lady who has led such a remarkable life.

　　Mrs. Wilson joins me in sending our warmest best wishes and our hope that you will continue to have good health, happiness and many more birthdays.

Sincerely,

Pete Wilson

STATE CAPITOL · SACRAMENTO, CALIFORNIA 95814

Wearing a white jacket bright with red cardinals, the gift of a dear friend, Hazel celebrates her 107th birthday November 22, 1997, on Daffodil Way, San Jose, California, where for the past twelve years she has made her home with her beloved daughter, Caroline Garrett.

"We tried to keep it low-key," Hazel wrote her publisher, "but with dozens of bouquets, gifts, boxes of chocolates, butterflies, and live lobsters flown in from Maine, it turned into a 'bash' after all!"

ONE HUNDRED AND SEVEN

As I reach one hundred and seven,
The time to depart will come soon.
My bag is packed! I'm ready for heaven!
I'll take coffee ice cream and my silver spoon.

A Scrabble game I know I'll need,
A funny story or two,
Poetry for something to read,
Memories of friends like you.

I'm ready to trade my rocking chair
For a pair of golden wings!
I'll soar aloft on currents of air
As a song of thanksgiving I sing!

During the last few weeks of Hazel's life, her daughter Caroline, nurses, and Hospice workers kept twenty-four-hour vigil by her bedside. Yvette Grigsby of Hospice tells us that a night or two before her death, Hazel whispered, "I used to write poems. I still want to write poems, but I can't any more. You write a poem for me."

This is the poem Yvette, who had never before written a line of verse, wrote and read to her patient – the amazing woman, Hazel Andrews Morrison, who nurtured, inspired, and blessed each one of us to the very end of her life and whose memory will continue to do so till the very end of ours.

SWEET BREATH OF LIFE
For a Precious Jewel

Mrs. Morrison, Mrs. Morrison,
Oh, how beautiful you look,
For God has shined His light on you.

Mrs. Morrison, Mrs. Morrison,
You don't have to worry,
For God has been faithful to you.

Mrs. Morrison, Mrs. Morrison,
Hold on fast, for Jesus is rocking you
In the bosom of His heart.

Mrs. Morrison, Mrs. Morrison,
Hold on to the faith,
For you're just one breath away
From the Sweet Savior, Your Lord in Christ.

Yvette Grigsby
January, 1998

78

Eternity

"It is eternity now.
I am in it. . . .
I am in it as the butterfly
        in the light-laden air. . . .
Now is eternity.
Now is the immortal life."

                        Richard Jeffries

A GLIMPSE OF PARADISE

Every morning I awaken
To a beautiful day —
Glorious when the sun shines,
Lovely when it's gray.
Cosy when it's raining,
Or when snowflakes fall —

But the day I find most thrilling,
Most exciting of them all,
Brings to mind a picture,
A glimpse of Paradise,
Where the crystal landscape
Wears a coat of sparkling ice.

HOMEWARD BOUND

So closely linked is earth to heaven
Sometimes I think I see
Dear ones who have gone before
Beckoning to me.

I know they will be waiting,
Eager to welcome me home.
Soon I shall hear them calling:
'She comes...she comes...she comes.'
1995

CIRCLES
Compo Beach
Westport, Connecticut

Pebbles we throw
In the stream of life
In widening circles blend,
Mingling with those
That have gone before,
For circles have no end.

Thus our living will surely be
Blended with eternity.

LOVE'S LEGACY

Three words live on in my heart,
Those you last spoke to me:
"Thank you, sweetheart," you said —
A heaven-sent legacy.

After that . . . eternity. . . .

REQUIEM

Someday I'll spread my earthbound wings
And fly to parts unknown.
No need for map or compass,
For I'll not fly alone.

God, who charted me through life,
Will lead the way for me,
And He will be my Guardian
Throughout eternity.

ABOUT THE AUTHOR

Hazel Grace Andrews, born a Connecticut Yankee in Bethel, CT, on November 22, 1890, graduated from Bethel High School and received a diploma in Normal Art and Manual Training from Pratt Institute in Brooklyn, NY. After five years' teaching experience in Sanford and Springvale, ME, she spent the next four years as Supervisor of Art in the Public Schools of Chicopee, MA.

In 1920 she married her high-school sweetheart, Garfield Morrison. Through busy years bringing up a daughter, Caroline, and two sons, Samuel and Sherman, she still found time for artistic expression, studying landscape painting with Bethel's noted artist, Charles A. Federer, water color with Alexander Crane, and early American decoration with Edith Fenner Wing of New Haven.

Church activities have also been an integral part of her life. In 1903 at age twelve, she joined the First Congregational Church in Bethel and is now, ninety-one years later, its oldest member.

In 1952, left alone by Garfield's untimely death, Hazel resumed her teaching career, opening a 'Kitchen Studio' in her Victorian home in Bethel. Here she taught Early American Decoration. Clients from all over Connecticut as well as from Pennsylvania and the mid-West flocked to her classes, relying on her expertise for restoration of tole ware, decorated furniture, and reverse painting on glass.

Much to Hazel's delight and surprise, these classes continued for the next thirty-five years until, at age ninety-five, Hazel left Bethel and moved to California. Here she makes her home with her daughter, Caroline Morrison Garrett and, with her genius for friendship, has a wide circle of friends.

She especially enjoys vists from nine grandchildren. Even though all nine were born, like Hazel, Connecticut Yankees, they come now, with spouses and seven great-grandchildren, from nine different states: Martha Veranth from Utah; Bill Morrison, Tennessee; Beth Morrison, Kansas; Nancy Morrison, Florida; Bob Morrison, Texas; Susan Jones, Virginia; Betsy Morrison, Colorado; Pamela Petro, California; and Rob Garrett, Oregon.

For creative fulfillment since coming to California, Hazel simply exchanged her brushes for her pen. With her continuing creativity, unfailing sense of humor, and zest for life, she has become a role model for graceful aging to all who reach 70, 80, 90, or even 100. Today as she nears her 104th birthday, wearing a sky-blue gown and an authentic butterfly scarf from the Smithsonian, she invites us to a signing party for her newly published book, *A Fluttering of Wings*, written for the most part since her 100th birthday.

The artistic motif of the book is, of course, the butterfly, symbol of the soul, the spirit. We salute the soul and the spirit of Hazel Andrews Morrison. Born in the 19th century, contributing to life generously and affirmatively throughout the 20th, here on the eve of the 21st century, this amazing woman is still creating beauty, still giving pleasure to her world.

"Didn't you know," she asks teasingly, "the 104th year is always the 'Year of the Butterfly'!"

CELEBRATING A BOOK AND A BIRTHDAY

"The embroidered tablecloth," Carol writes, "is ironed; the gold-edged, hand-painted china washed and sparkling. Blue butterfly placecards fly high over beautiful new blue books, and Mother is wearing her butterfly scarf. All is in readiness for the gala birthday-book-signing party."

Hazel Andrews Morrison
November 22, 1994
104th Birthday Party

From the author:

Every day *A Fluttering of Wings* brings new surprises that magnify the beauty and joy of living.

Butterflies are in every room of my house — stained glass, stone, crystal, paper, brass.

Every day I give thanks to God for giving me friends to round out His plan for my life.

Hazel Andrews Morrison

From the publisher:

That an artist should write verse at all is unusual. Gifted in non-verbal media, few artists are writers.

That an artist should publish a first book of verse at age 104 is even more unusual.

That the first printing of that book should sell out and a second printing be ordered in exactly one month is most unusual of all— almost a kind of publishing miracle. Few books of verse ever go into a second printing.

Yet this is the story of *A Fluttering of Wings* by Hazel Andrews Morrison. "My life," Hazel, amazed by the response to her book, exclaims delightedly, "had died down to a few smoldering embers. Clarine came along and poured on gasoline."

84

"If a butterfly," physicists tell us, "flutters its wings in Tokyo, the effect will be felt two weeks later in weather patterns in New York City." Hazel's book has had something of this 'butterfly effect,' the fluttering of its pages felt back and forth across the country in hundreds of homes and hundreds of hearts. People read one copy of the book, then call to order 5, 10, 15 more.

So—here is the second printing and a few comments from the many phone calls and letters Hazel and the publisher have received.

Clarine Coffin Grenfell, Director
Grenfell Reading Center, Orland, ME

From the readers:

"Hooray! It's wonderful! A toast to the author! A toast to the editor! And a toast to the printer! Hazel is one of the very few people I will ever meet who can so clearly articulate both verbally and pictorially her thoughts, feelings, and ideas. What a gift!"
Penny Havard, Rowayton, CT

"Have read the book from cover to cover and am amazed by it. 'Lovely' is too poor a word to describe it . . . Hazel, always retain your philosophy of life — the love, happiness, and joy which show so well in your poetry.
Charles L. Steeves, Stratford, CT

"Every Friday afternoon I pick up my four-year-old grandson, Matthew, for an hour's drive to stay overnight with Grandpa and Grandma. Along the way we often play tapes.
" 'Want to listen to a tape of poetry?' I asked him yesterday, 'They're mostly nature poems — read by a friend of mine.' Matthew agreed excitedly. He clapped his hands at 'Low Tide' and after 'Choice' agreed he'd like to be a lightning bug — if he were ever a bug! As I turned the tape, he said, 'Your friend has a nice, singing voice, Grandma.' Amazing that a woman 104 can write verses to please a child of 4! A hundred years apart!"
Jean Hagan, Warren, RI

"I was expecting quiet, nostalgic remembrances. Surprise! Vigorous humor makes *A Fluttering of Wings* startling and strong . . . a unique talent!"
Dorothy Harte, Palm Springs, CA

"What a wonderful signing party — butterflies, books, laughs and fun! What more could anyone ask? I am delighted with the book."
Eva Tatum, Los Gatos, CA

"Hazel Morrison's book reveals clearly the integrity of a life well-lived — childhood, youth, maturity, old age fitting together in a matchless way. The book appeals to all ages. Daughter Trevanna (10) and son Trevanion (8) laughed uproariously at the contrast between the stereotyped old woman dressed in black, 'sipping cambric tea to comfort me,' and Hazel's older woman of the '90's 'longing to model those tight-fitting jeans.'

"My wife Linda and I enjoyed the winking moon in 'Romance at 102.' What an affirmation of the undying spirit of romance in each of us! My family had never heard of Hazel Morrison, but we felt moved to telephone her and enjoyed a half-hour of delightful conversation."
Dr. John Millard Grenfell, Director
Family Counseling Center, Skowhegan, ME

"You can't imagine the excitement the announcement of your new notoriety caused at Travelers Club! We have enjoyed the poems and especially the pictures! You are an inspiration! We have ordered more copies."
Margaret Hoyt, Bethel, CT

"*A Fluttering of Wings* arrived this week and enriched not only my life but the life of everyone with whom I've shared your verses. The entire presentation is beautiful. . . . Reading the Foreword, I was surprised to learn your publisher and 'persuader' lives nearby in Orland — phoned to thank her and had a most enjoyable chat. I told her your 'Kitchen Studio' nourished not only creativity but also the soul. Those hours were great thereapy because you shared so much of yourself."
Norma Simard, Winterport, ME

"I have spent beautiful moments reading your poems, although my English is not so good anymore. I very much appreciate your sense of humor and your sensibility. It is gracefulness to have this way of expression, this freedom with words."
Annette Desgraz, Montreux, Switzerland

"I sat down with my cup of tea and read your poetry. It took me away to a simpler, more innocent time when life was not so complicated and hectic. Thank you for sharing your poetry and life with us. What a wonderful gift — one I will cherish all my life!"
Terry Bailey, Fort Smith, AR

"What a delightful book! Everything about it is charming. What beautiful pictures you have painted with your poems! You are truly one of the GREATS! Your values, wisdom, wit, and creativity will continue to be an encouragement to all whose lives you touch — a rich heritage for your family through all the circling years!"
Jerry and Alma Lamb, La Mesa, CA

"I am so thrilled with your wonderful book and so proud of you and your poetry! Your dedication to your daughter Carol is so loving! . . . John and I sat in our living room and listened to Clarine reading. She does it so well! I will write and thank her for urging you to do this lovely work — my best Christmas present this year. I shall treasure it always."
Audrey Stryker, Brookfield Center, CT

"What a thrill to have your book of verse — a lovely glimpse of a long, remarkable life. Flutterings, indeed!"
Nilla Palmer, Waterford, CT

"Saturday night Kerney called me out to look at the beautiful full moon. We saw him wink — but knew it was really for a beautiful person in California getting ready to celebrate her 104th birthday! It brought smiles to us because we knew she was probably winking back!"
Kathleen McCormick, Houston, TX

"Thank you for your beautiful book, *A Fluttering of Wings*. I know my statements must be repetitious of others you've received, but you deserve oceans of accolades. You are an inspiration to all ages. Not only have you shown the rewards of enjoying life, but you have merged your artistic and verbal skills to paint word pictures of nature, feelings, and tributes to loved ones and to the varied stages of a meaningful life. . . .
"It will be my pleasure to profile you and your book!"
Ethel Kessler, San Jose, CA

"*A Fluttering of Wings* is wonderful! Don't know when I've enjoyed a book so much and had such fun sharing it! Today at my Bridge Club meeting it's going to be a star! One member, June Preston, is a true authority on butterflies. She and her husband have a much larger collection than KU's Science Museum. I told her there's more to butterflies than she ever guessed and that I'd show her today! Fun!"
                    Virginia Meserve, Lawrence, KS

"Now Hazel reaches a hundred and four.
Wow! Do we need to still keep score?
You've blessed so many — your joy's alive!
Now, press on to a hundred and five!"
                    Donald Cantrell, San Jose, CA

"I sat down and read the entire book as soon as I received it. . . . Your sense of humor and descriptions of nature especially appeal to me. My particular favorite is 'Low Tide' — personally meaningful, as summers at Compo Cove were among the happiest times of my life. Am sending to Maine for three copies of the book for my boys."
                    Shirley Long, Kentfield, CA

"A joyful experience to walk alongside you on your rich and eventful 104-year journey. we also got some real good laughts!"
                    Rev. Philip Jordan, Fresno, CA

"Thank you, thank you for making it possible for Hazel to have *A Fluttering of Wings* published! It is most delightful. I laugh and I cry with it as I used to do sitting at Hazel's lunch table. I, too, was one who painted with her and loved every minute of it. My favorite possessions are those I painted with her. . . ."
                    Helen Platt Tornillo, Hendersonville, NC

"I listened to the tape *A Fluttering of Wings* on my way to work at the area's Adult Day Care and was mesmerized by the voice! Each poem brought me a different emotion . . . an inspirational tape and book. . . . We will have another order for you after our next UMW meeting."
                    Madeline Aragones, Newtown, CT

"What a wonderful treasure! Especially love 'In Style at Ninety' and 'Romance at 102!' Can't wait to have the verse from 105!"
Ann Walden, Danbury, CT

"Dear Grandmother,
Happy 104th! Not many grandchildren get to write that! Your book is a wonderful hit with everyone. You are becoming a celebrity in Udall, Kansas. Not many grandchildren get to write that, either! Hope your birthday is terrific — if we could be with you, we would.

Beth Morrison   Jane Shirley
Udall, KA   Cary, NC

"Thank you, thank you for the beautiful book! I will treasure it as long as I live — can't tell you how much I enjoyed reading it and know I will be reading it again and again. You are an inspiration to all us lesser mortals, a special 'one of a kind!' "
Cathie Groundwater, Southington, CT

"My friends all call me a 'Butterfly Nut,' so here is my check for three copies of the book Grenfell Reading has just published — two for my 'Butterfly Nut' friends and one for me!"
Gladys Hart, Fort Lauderdale, FL

"I have just received my treasured and much anticipated copy of my grandmother's book, *A Fluttering of Wings*. It turned out beautifully. Thank you so much for making it all possible! Please send additional copies as soon as possible. The family is, once again so proud of my beloved grandmother!"
Nancy Morrison, West Palm Beach, FL

Just called a friend . . .
I chose to adopt her
As my telephonic
Lepidopter.
Her rainbow of poems
Keeps me trying.
No one will stop
Our butterflying!
Richard Morton, West Hartford, CT

A Sampling of Reader Response to 3rd Printing:

"The highlight of my trip to California was meeting Hazel Andrews Morrison and her daughter Caroline Garrett in their beautiful home, filled with antiques. Here my friend Grace Davenport and I stand with Hazel before a priceless silk quilt used as a wall hanging."
                    Gladys Hart, Fort Lauderdale, FL

"Grenfell Reading Center: I would like to order two more copies of a wonderful book you published a year ago, *A Fluttering of Wings* by Hazel Morrison. It brought magic and delight into my life and I am hoping it is still available.   Also — is it still possible to order a copy of *Women My Husband Married* by Clarine Coffin Grenfell?

"Last year I sent Mrs. Morrison a birthday card and I am hoping she is still alive so I can send her another in November of this year for her 106th.   I received a lovely letter in response from Mrs. Morrison's daughter, plus three wonderful verses from the poetess herself. I felt very honored! I enclose a check."
                    Loy Mitchell, Palo Alto, CA

"Thank you for copyright permission to reprint "The Butterfly Ballet" in the November *Newsletter* from *H.O.M.E.* I have your tape in my car and play it often — it is read so beautifully. Here is my check for another copy of your book for my niece in Germany."

Dorothy Schwarzkopf, Middletown, CT

"I have just read a friend's copy of *A Fluttering of Wings*. It was like seeing some of my own verse in print! Our words are different, but subjects and even the meter are the same. I, too, live by the sea. Please send a copy for me."

Thomasina Pritchard Rush, Brookings, OR

"Dear Hazel, Thank you for sharing your optimism with the world. My mother is 83 and in good health, but talks as though she has little to live for. You set an example that we have so much to look forward to each day. Your gift to the world will be my mother's Mother's Day gift from me. Here's to your health, faith, optimism, and to your continued work."

Carla Griffin, San Jose, CA

"When the Good Lord created Lady Hazel, He should have continued using the same mold several million times. What a beautiful and loving world this would be! The recipe for the mold would include Honesty, Compassion, Truthfulness, Ambition, Thoughtfulness and loads of Love. My notepaper is too small! This list could go on and on!"

Lee Yetter, Danbury, CT

"*A Fluttering of Wings* is sheer delight! It is a joy and comfort to me to handle this precious book — absolutely amazing when so many people during their 'golden years' are quite satisfied to fade away. You have lived a colorful, productive life and are now enhancing your readers' lives. May God shower upon you His choicest blessings."

Eva Durst, Bristol, RI

"Thank you for leaving us your legacy of knowledge and wisdom. They will remain in our thoughts forever and will be from one generation to the next generation. The book is very inspiring and I can visualize your poetry clearly. May God bless you and I pray you will have more birthdays to come. In Christ's Name,"

Marina Sanpani, Sunnyvale, CA

"The picture of your home in Bethel and your poem "A Teacher's Heart" brought back many happy memories of when I was a learner in your 'Kitchen Studio.' I still have and treasure some trays, a rocker and chair that I painted with your encouragement. With your faith in God, your wonderful sense of humor and *joie de vivre*, your words will leave a lasting impression on the hearts of family and friends — a precious legacy to all."

Nancy Lucas, Fort Myers, FL

"This week at Friends' House Pre-School Michael O'Brien brought his grandmother, Jean Hagen, to read your poetry. The children and teachers both enjoyed this experience very much. Later the children drew the enclosed pictures based on your poem 'Low Tide.' They wanted to thank you for your beautiful poetry. Thank you for sharing your wonderful gift!"

Friends' House Pre-School, Warwick, RI

"My mother sent me your book this Christmas and I would like to let you know it is one of the nicest gifts I received. I read every word from cover to cover and thoroughly enjoyed it. . . . I think the book is put together beautifully and I congratulate you on its success. I would like to send you one of my poems:

"Treasure
Each new day —
For each holds
Its own memory.

As the days drift by —
The memories blossom
Like wild flowers
Brightly colored,
Sweetly scented

Some to travel with the breeze —
Spreading joy where they land —
Others remain
To be gathered and pressed
In volumes
Within our hearts."

Denise McQuiston, Faucett, MO

"*A Fluttering of Wings* is a refreshing look at a wonderful life. Thank you for sharing it with me."
                    Dr. Robert H. Schuller, Garden Grove, CA

"*A Fluttering of Wings* is such a great book that I want to order three more books and one tape. I have a cousin who is now finishing a book and I'm going to send him a copy and tell him not to give up. He still has 50 years of writing to equal the longevity of Hazel Morrison!"
                    Ken Johnson, Apple Valley, CA

"Your book of poetry is an inspiration for every age group. You will be getting many orders from my Valley Health Network Caregivers. My friend Betsy gave one to her mother, who was very depressed over her 100th birthday, had no energy to do anything except stay in bed and little will left to go on.

"After receiving your book, her attitude changed. Your book has given her the inspiration and will to go on. She has more energy. She wants to participate in life. She is a changed person. Her daughter is pleased and finds she has her mother back!

"I wish my son's school would use your poetry. The poems can start many discussions about life which I think would help eighth-graders immensely, since it is a time of many changes for them. Thank you for writing this book!"
                    Sally Ryan, Sunnyvale, CA

"Congratulations to you for showing the rest of us how to stay healthy in mind and body. You are an inspiration to anyone who has a problem enjoying life on this magnificent planet. We read about your remarkable life in the feature story by Ethel Kessler in the *San Jose Mercury News*."
                    Keith and Darlene Thaxton, Los Altos, CA

"We wish you continued success in the publication and marketing of your writing. Thank you for confirming our belief that self-publishing is both a vital and increasingly appropriate option for today's writer and one that's fully capable of rivaling the best productions of the commercial publishing establishment."
                    Thomas Clark, Editor
                    Writer's Digest
                    Cincinnati, OH

"*A Fluttering of Wings* sounds like fun — and inspiring for someone who had begun to feel old at 72! Many thanks!"
                    Charlotte Kitouski, Florence, MA

"Someone sent me your book as a gift and I want you to know I have read it from cover to cover with delight and awe. Although it is hard to choose, I think my favorite poem is 'Riches.' The entire collection with the wonderful pictures records so beautifully a life that has truly made the most of very special gifts and made this world a better, happier place. It will always be a treasure to me and a real inspiration. I am very grateful."
Susan Snead, Camden, ME

"I am always thrilled to find 'kindred spirits' in reading or meeting others. Mrs. Morrison has charming expression and makes me wish, 'Why didn't I think to word my thoughts that way!' "
Sonya Seigal, Amsterdam, NY

"Re: *A Fluttering of Wings:*
    Your poetry is a treasure
    And it modulates with pleasure!
Please send two more copies."
Ed Defreitas
Farmington, CT

"Thank you for your part in the quality of my mother's life in her last several months. *A Fluttering of Wings* was on her table with her Bible . . . when she died, a bookmark on page 46, noting, I believe, the little poem 'Today's the Day.' "
The Rev. Richard Evans, Boston, MA

"All Hazel's friends in Bethel were delighted with Hazel's book and thoroughly enjoyed reading it. Please tell her I am sending another box of chocolate lace candy (made here in Bethel) for her 106th birthday."
Eleanor Sutton, Bethel, CT

"Your book is such a delight! I've read it through at least five times myself and outloud to others. It is just a beautiful book! I must say I admire your picture with the butterfly scarf! I used to read John Ciardi's book, *I'll Read to You — You Read to Me* to my son by the hour. In college my favorite poet was Edna St. Vincent Millay. I have no aspirations to write poetry, but I do love to read it. Thank you for your most beautiful book and the tape."
Pat Butterfoss, Cherry Hill, NJ

"Wonderful book! Great lady!"
Suzanne C. Betterley, Worcester, MA

From the Publisher:

Almost from its first day of publication in 1994 *A Fluttering of Wings* has aroused a tremendous response among its readers. Many reorders come to Grenfell Reading Center accompanied by words of praise, which we forward to Hazel. She thoroughly enjoys reading her 'fan mail' and often responds with new verses of appreciation. Thus bridges of friendship are built between writer and readers.

Very often these readers are young children, so let us close this fourth printing with one example of such remarkable communication between the nearly 106-year-old poet and 6-year-old boys and girls, students of Adele Ames in Capri School, Brewer, Maine. Each fall Mrs. Ames teaches the first-graders to identify the monarch chrysalis, bring any they find to their classroom, then count the days until the monarchs emerge and begin their long journey from Maine to southern California.

This fall Mrs. Ames introduced the children to Hazel's poems, especially *The Butterfly Ballet*, which they decided to dramatize. They liked the picture of Hazel and her little sister Pauline and wondered if Pauline, too, had lived to be 100 years old. They decided to write Hazel a letter. She responded with a copy of her book for each one of them and a poem:

BUTTERFLY FRIENDS

When the postman brought the mail,
    Imagine my surprise—
The biggest letter I'd ever seen!
    I couldn't believe the size!

The butterfly drawing amazed me.
    How special each name on the wings!
Mrs. Ames must be a great teacher
    To think of such wonderful things.

I am truly impressed
    That you like *Butterfly Ballet*.
You've chosen my very own favorite,
    And I write poems every day.

How I wish I could tell you
    My sister is still alive.
She died many years ago
    When she was eighty-five.

You ask about my birthday.
It is seven weeks away.
November the twenty-second
Will be the exciting day.

There will be dozens of candles,
Cards and presents, too.
I am going to be one-hundred-and-six—
One hundred years older than you.

California is home to the monarchs.
Each winter they come back again—
A constant reminder how lucky I am
To have butterfly friends in Maine!

For Grade 1, Capri School, Brewer, Maine
San Jose, California, October 15, 1996

Mrs. Ames continues this 'fan-letter' story:

"The children were so *very* excited today when they received a reply from Hazel. We had written to ask if her sister Pauline were still alive. (Keegan wanted to know.) Hazel sent a book to every child in the class, wrote a poem for the occasion, and sent *us* a thank-you card! We were very touched.

"Our principal, Cathy Lewis, had to use two of my kleenex to get through the poem! It is called *Butterfly Friends* and it just so happens that is the name of our Butterfly Garden. (Coincidence—God's way of remaining anonymous!) In it Hazel talks about her birthday November 22. We are planning something special for her—a surprise. I wish I had video-taped the children while I read the poem and passed out the books. The *Butterfly Ballet* was quickly found on page 31. What an exciting afternoon! Life is good."

Fifty . . . sixty . . . seventy years from now, can you hear some man or woman telling a grandchild: "See this old book of poems? It was a present when I was six years old. . . A poet named Hazel sent it to me from California. And here's the first poem I ever learned by heart, about butterflies. Our teacher dressed us up like monarchs and we did a ballet. . . ."

Yes, publishing what Hazel Andrews Morrison calls her 'little verses' and reading her 'fan mail' have both been fun from beginning to end. Undoubtedly Hazel's most endearing characteristic—and perhaps the trait that has kept her young in heart for 106 years—is her irrepressible sense of humor, her love of a good joke, whether on herself or someone else. Tell her some incident you found embarrassing or upsetting or even tragic. Then, a day or so later, find in your mailbox the same incident touched by Hazel's wit, retold in the verses that continue to flow so easily from her amazingly creative brain. Suddenly you, too, see the funny side, the ridiculous, and start laughing.

Last week such an incident happened here at Grenfell Reading Center in tiny Orland—population 1500, one store, one church, one industry, a huge paper mill. Let me share it with you, thus closing Hazel's book as she would want us to do—laughing at ourselves, seeing the ridiculous side, enjoying this wonderful life—in short, having fun.

Clarine Coffin Grenfell, Director
Grenfell Reading Center, Orland, Maine

CLARINE'S LATRINES
Best Place in Town

Orland buzzed with anticipation,
The whole town caught up in preparation
For three thousand people arriving today
For Champion's Race and Clarine's Book Display.

Mill officials and town committee
Plan details to handle the crowd from the city—
Some coming to cheer the Knock-out Race,
Some to buy books at the Grenfell Place.

For Africa U. in far-off Zimbabwe
Has empty shelves in its new library,
While Clarine has a plan that cannot fail—
On the day of the Race, a Big Book Sale!

She invites all her friends and asks them to dine
On her flowered porch opposite the Finish Line.
Now they stare in surprise at the Reverend's home,
While she looks on with a face of doom,

Appalled by a sight not made in heaven—
  Leading up to her porch, latrines, numbered seven!
Call "Public Relations" a solution to find—
  And also to give them a piece of her mind!

All agree! "The location's a grievous mistake!
  What can we do to compensate?"
"For these hideous boxes? Pay rent for my land!"
  (Africa U. needs a helping hand.)

"Fifty's my price for each of the seven!"
  A check does the trick, and all is forgiven.
People rush by the hundreds all day to Clarine's,
  Desperate to use the handy latrines.

She greets each one with a welcoming look,
  Then graciously sells them an armload of books.
Fame comes to Orland, but not from the Race,
  Potty Row proved to be the most popular place.

H.A.M.
September 15, 1996

FAN MAIL

Thank you for the pleasure
*   Your letters give to me!*
How I wish that I could answer
*   Each one separately!*

Mail comes from near and far.
*   Each week brings more and more,*
Revealing friends I'll never meet —
*   The list grows by the score!*

Though I may never see you,
*   This greeting is sincere:*
Your loving response to my verses
*   Is a treasure I hold dear!*

1996

ORDERING INFORMATION

Please order directly from the publisher or the distributor:

CLARINE G. GRENFELL, PUBLISHER
P. O. Box 98, Orland, ME 04472-0098
Tel: 1-207-469-7102   Email: clarine@aol.com

CAROLINE GARRETT, DISTRIBUTOR
BUTTERFLY BOOKS
23500 Cristo Rey Drive, Apt. 413E
Cupertino, CA 95014-6532
Tel: 1-650-210-9440

In print: single copy $12.50 + $2.50 S&H
(Total $15.00) ISBN 0-9612766-4-9

On tape: single 90-minute cassette $10.00 + $2.50 S&H
(Total $12.50) ISBN 0-9612766-6-5

Special combination offer:
Book & Tape $22.50
Free shipping & handling

State of California residents ordering from CA please add $7\frac{3}{4}\%$
sales tax.
MAKE CHECK PAYABLE TO CAROLINE GARRETT
or to CLARINE C. GRENFELL

Orders are filled on the day received, sent first-class mail, and
may be sent (as gifts) to a different address.

PLEASE PRINT ALL NAMES & ADDRESSES.